W9-DBX-667

IF I DREAM

I HAVE YOU,

I HAVE YOU

IF I DREAM

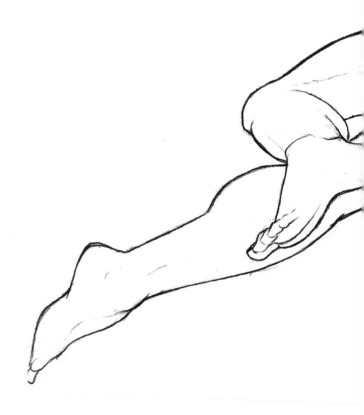

I HAVE YOU,

I HAVE YOU

Poems by RICHARD HOWARD

Drawings by John Button

TIBOR DE NAGY EDITIONS

NEW YORK   1997

First Edition published in 1997 by
Tibor de Nagy Editions
724 Fifth Avenue
New York, NY 10019

All poems in this book have been published previously.

ISBN 1-891123-50-5

CONTENTS

III.

INTRODUCTION

I am looking, as I write, at an unpaged pamphlet of poems by John Ashbery—it was his first publication, *Turandot and Other Poems*—with four drawings by Jane Freilicher, identified rather grandly as "Editions of the Tibor de Nagy Gallery," printed "under the supervision of Nell Blaine" and dated 1953. At intervals, over the decades that followed, John Myers printed, under the gallery's auspices, a number of such broadsides, leaflets and chapbooks, which turn out to have been—for such was his taste and his triumphant identification of poetry as well as of painting, his enthusiastic sense of what work in the arts was lively and likely to sustain our attention—of permanent interest, even (from a collector's point of view) of permanent value: I am holding on to *Turandot*, with its penciled dedication by the poet, against the necessities of Bad Times to Come.

It is a great pleasure to resume the series with John Button's drawings and some poems of mine, in tribute to John Myers' memory, or rather to his nourishing energy as it functioned through, around, and in a sense under the Tibor de Nagy Gallery: not even Frank O'Hara was such an animator of the arts, these last forty years, as John proved to be, and indeed it is his memory that suggests the happy continuation of these tracts for the times, confident in the assumption that some poems and some pictures might join forces to mutual advantage, a reminder of the pleasures afforded by such informal yet fervent manifestations.

— RICHARD HOWARD

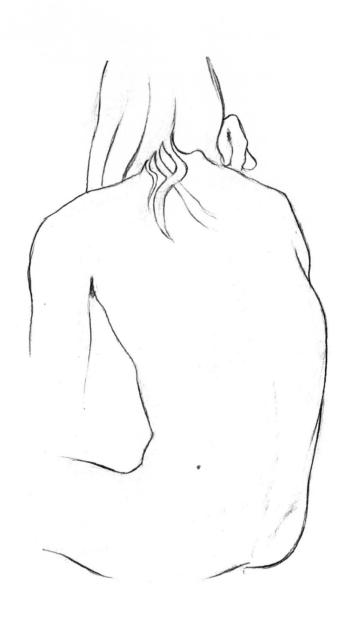

I.

The Difference

Looking at you
I cannot help surmising
   As I admire the view
That a landscape so enticing
   Must be also true.

Cast in their unwrinkled case,
   The apportionment
Of featured precincts in your face
   Surely represents
A genuine genius of the place.

But looking at me
I find it hard believing
   Myself is what I see
—As if by merely moving
   My face might get free

Of what is nothing more than some
   Irrelevant mask.
On you it's you, and even dumb
   Owns what I must ask:
Mine the foreign parts, yours home.

At Compo Beach

Drastic in its claims upon
Our two-dimensioned holiday
Where sea and sky so neatly hinge,

Your body standing in the sun
Becomes a site of sudden change,
Accuses where we would applaud,

And criticizes every hour
Of light with shadows adequate
To prove the flattened air a fraud.

You walk across the stony beach,
Appropriately negligent
Of effort, and in spite of each

Inhuman task I summon up
To justify men being here,
Facility, I see, is all:

Where one tall bather is enough
To be our season's Centaur, just
By wading slowly out to where

The sea's green fur begins at length
To grow against you, and your own
Accustomed skin gives way to end

In a flourish of salt, swart hair.
How well the unsaddled ocean serves
As stallion half to the human beast!

And for the time we idly stare,
You leave Connecticut behind
With an obsolete shirt and socks and us

On shore—to join the heroes you
Have never heard of in the sea,
Irrelevant as any myth

To all our merely human loves.

Do It Again:
Didactic Stanzas

i   Being! Being! the body rants
When pain is the color of certain events:
    Surely it's better to scream "I suffer"
    Than say "This landscape is ugly."

ii   Comes a time, in the dead of doubt,
When action alone is certainty:
    The heart's still-lifes are still
    Only after a violent death.

iii   Pale in the prospect of my love
Your body lies, a fiction but
    My one chance of saving what
    Time and society erode.

iv   So I return to the gestures of lust
As if it were to innocence:
    Repetition is the only mode
    That nature knows of memory.

209 *Canal*

Not hell but a street, not
Death but a fruit-stand, not
Devils just hungry devils
Simply standing around the stoops, the stoops.

We find our way, wind up
The night, wound uppermost,
In four suits, a funny pack
From which to pick ourselves a card, any card:

Clubs for beating up, spades
For hard labor, diamonds
For buying up rough diamonds,
And hearts, face-up, face-down, for facing hearts.

Dummies in a rum game
We count the tricks that count
Waiting hours for the dim bar
Like a mouth to open wider After Hours.

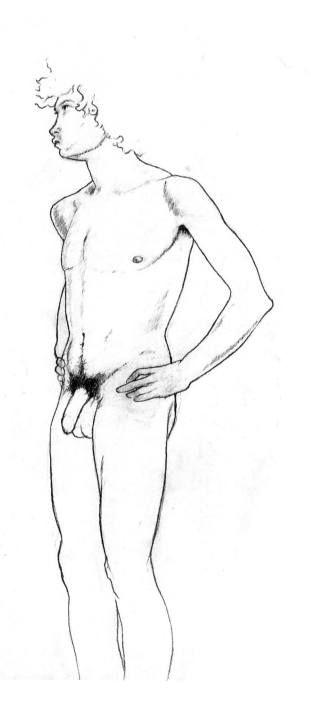

On Hearing Your Lover Is Going
to the Baths Tonight

Does it matter? Do you mind?
Here, now, is an opportunity for Mind
over Matter, the one triumph: whatever
    in life we really accept
undergoes a change, the world is not the same—
    a quality is added,
        everything has its shadow.
As for *minding*, now's your chance: what easier
        occasion for opening
letters (not those from you) like so many wounds,
finding literal motives for being left
    in the lurch . . . what *is* a lurch?
Before you start spying for real, consider
        what is wrong here, or who wronged?
        Name one man (you included)
whose venery, given vent, has failed to be
        venereal in bringing
home the old surrealist bacon: tireless
pursuit of the Same New Thing! What do you have
        to complain about? Having
things your own way is not really having them:
        jealousy is out, as Proust
        has taken some pains to prove.
It has nothing to do with love, jealousy,
        it is only passed around
at the same time, like pepper with the melon,
for people who happen not to know better:

anyone who knows melon
would never touch it. Your fantasy of his
    body doing what it does
    with yours, only doing so
with others. . . is *that* the difficulty? Then
    put yourself at ease: two mouths
have never drunk twice from the same chimera.
What he does with you is you; with others, them:
    "he" remains a mystery—
you personify only what you are not,
    and you are not there. Be glad;
that is a world diminished to an often-
catalogued repository of objects,
    possessing no absolute
and final face, no recognitions. There is
    (Keats has the words) no wonder
    but the human face. What is
that face except our body trying to be
    more naked than the body?
Where better than in the dripping faceless dark
for him to discover, and discard, himself,
    returning then, rinsed free. . .
All the terminations belong to others,
    time alone is yours. Alone.

Among The Missing

Know me? I am the ghost of Gansevoort Pier.
  Out of the Trucks, beside the garbage scow
  where rotten pilings form a sort of prow,
I loom, your practiced shadow, waiting here

for celebrants who cease to come my way,
  though mine were limbs as versatile as theirs
  and eyes as vagrant. Odd that no one cares
to ogle me now where I, as ever, lay

myself out, all my assets and then some,
  weather permitting. Is my voice so faint?
  Can't you hear me over the river's complaint?
Too dark to see me? Have you all become

ghosts? What earthly good is that? I want
  incarnate lovers hungry for my parts,
  longing hands and long-since lonely hearts!
It is your living bodies I must haunt,

and while the Hudson hauls its burdens past,
  having no hosts to welcome or repel
  disclosures of the kind I do so well,
I with the other ghosts am I laid at last.

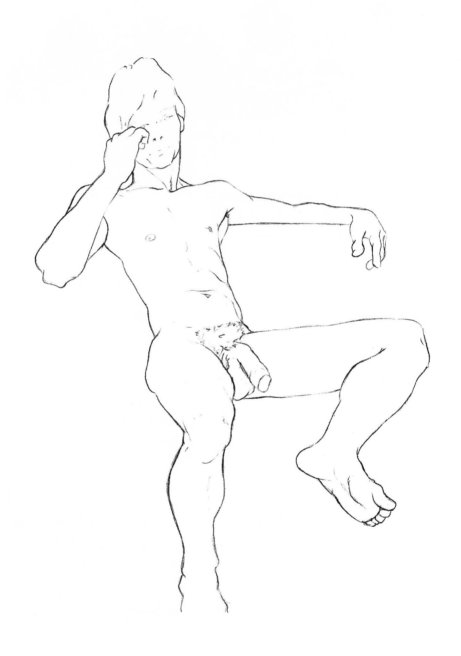

II.

"Richard, What Will It Be Like When
You Ask the Questions?"

Like a landscape by night, and in summer, riding
the ghost of a road (or what you take for a road,
wet still and hissing under your bicycle tires
    after an afternoon's rain),
but the ground keeps rising, the gray cumulus thins,
and there is the moon! round and sudden in the sky
like an old sun casting a sort of dead daylight
    upon the world's premises,
cancelling shadowy promises of escape
at a slowed tempo of resignation, so that
there is no story left to tell yourself or me
    about the Day that Never
or about the Night that Always—no story now
about what had been or what would be—it is how
you become a storyteller: there is no story,
    so you have to make it up.
Even the same actions differ when repeated;
this one will be the same, but with a difference
more interesting than the sameness, which is
    more significant than
the difference. You will find it matters little
whether noon or the false noon of moonlight fastens
your shadow to the macadam, whether you put
    questions or are put to them,
loser, you will find there is nothing to choose,
whether you make others suffer or prefer them
to inflict suffering on you: it is always
    a god being crucified.

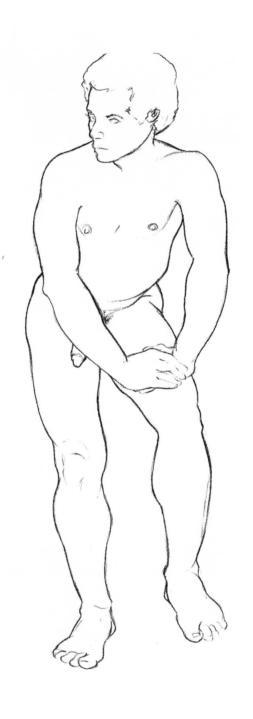

"Richard, We Were Here Before,
Don't You Remember?"

I remember how the valley turned from umber
to burnt sienna, how the clouds above Siena
 broke their Tuscan habit
of harboring grudges—it came down that morning
as if nothing would be held or held back again!
 But we were never there.
I remember the road Rocamadour turning
round until it was ready to make a run for
 the hills overhanging
a chateau caramel in the afternoon light.
I remember how you took one hand from the wheel
 and your new driving-glove
was the same caramel. You turned, like the valley
or like the road, and I remember your face then,
 but it never happened.
And your face now, now we are here and our hostess
shows us to the same table we shared last time
 in Ye Waverly Inn
—I forget your face. "Last time" is no more than lost,
a series of revelations leading up to
 a full-length mirror,
and only my fictions can free me from myself.
Liberation is never complete while life "lasts",
 and nothing afterward.

"Richard, Isn't There a Good Movie
We Could Go Out To?"

Out? I keep going in to mine, the blue kind
You come in the middle of. But then, you are
    Color blind, and not to blame.
Your memory for figures must be as bad
As a mirror's, or is it too dark in here?
    The best features have moved on:
What merely happens passes, and what never
Happens is eternal—perpetual motion
    Pictures. Camera! Action!
It *is* a good movie I am watching here
In which I began as its only actor, end
    As its only audience.

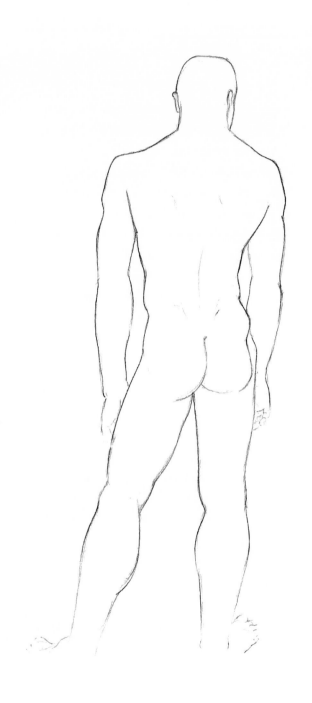

"Richard, May I Ask A Horrible Question? Isn't It Painful When Two Men Make Love Together?"

There is a horrible answer, to part of it—when
two men make love apart, that is the most painful.
Remember what I say—it may come up again.
　　But you mean something else:
bodies whose engineering has failed to manage
or match their architecture, in which case Power
gets no good out of Form, or only the better
　　of Form. Is that what you mean?
There is a solution (*I* mean, it is soluble):
you concentrate upon the parts and let the whole
take care of itself. Anyway, what about pain?
　　Is there pain and not-pain?
Or is there the discovery that they become
each other when you traverse a certain terrain?
It is like electricity, pain: not a thing
　　but the way things behave.
Behaving yourself, then, is a way of having
yourself be; pain a manner (sometimes a Grand one),
not what is the matter. Merely signifying,
　　it is insignificant.

A body of knowledge. As I know best now,
Regarding yours across the abyss between
    That chair and this one,
My ignorance the kind of bliss unlikely
To bridge the furniture without a struggle,
    A scene—mad or bad
Or just gauche. The known body is Greek to me,
Though I am said to have conspicuous gifts
    As a translator.
More likely the Bible is the right version:
All knowledge was probably gained at first hand
    And second nature;
To know the Lord was to be flesh of His flesh.
There was a God, but He has been dismembered;
    We are the pieces.

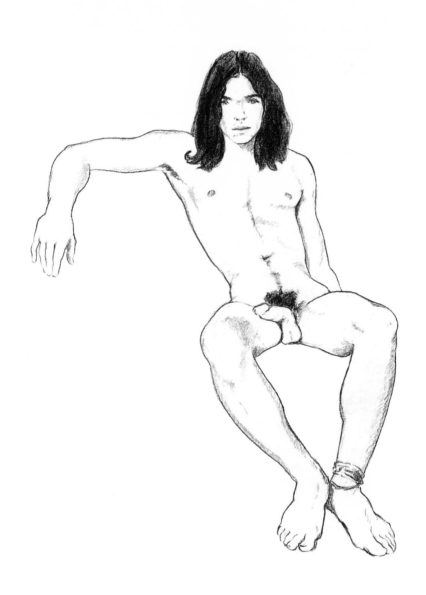

"Richard, May I Ask You Something?
Is Poetry Involved with Evil?"

If we follow Sade (as we do, from a distance—
After all, who could keep up?) the Law is crime's cause,
    Wedlock the source of divorce,
Nor can any Garden grow till we acknowledge
The weeds suffered outside, not sadistically,
    Just dialectically.
So much, then, for "involvement": no *Paradiso*
Without, in poetry at least, infernal parts.
    But let the word itself speak—
Evil, from Indo-European roots, flowers
Like a weed, meaning "up-from-under" and "over"
    (as *eaves* drop from above us)
Meaning also "supine", "thrown-backward" and "under",
Meaning, as roots so often seem to mean, its own
    Opposite besides itself.
There we have it, as *I* would have it: infernal
Parts beside themselves, opposites supine, so that
    As even this four-letter
Old-English word means, *we* can be "extended forms
Which signify *exceeding the proper limit.*"
    Flowers of excess—O good!

"Afterwards, Richard, What Will We Do ?
What Will We Say?"

When you work the mirror over, prying for signs,
perhaps it will come as a surprise that there are
    none to be found in the glass.
What we do leaves no trace on others, what is done
to us, none on ourselves: so much for principles.
    Kissing is not cosmetic,
merely cosmic, and even after there has been
breaking and entering, everyone's flesh is opaque
    to the feelings of others.
A given body takes time, like a good burglar,
and cleans up after itself. Nothing our hands do
    discharges our heart's behavior,
yet the change will be there, you are right about that,
though wrong to look for it where you do: there will be
    no revealing scars—nothing
shows up except what is shown up to be nothing,
standing for what cannot be said or done now,
    or not standing for such things
another minute, representative but intolerant.
Before, what we did not do or say found its sense
    or subsistence—livelihood—
in the unlived life. From here on in, a likeness
alone remains, a semblance of the unspeakable.
    So little is to be learned
from our fashions of making love, even from passions:
our faces do not show the past, they face our fate.
    Every sentence has been earned.

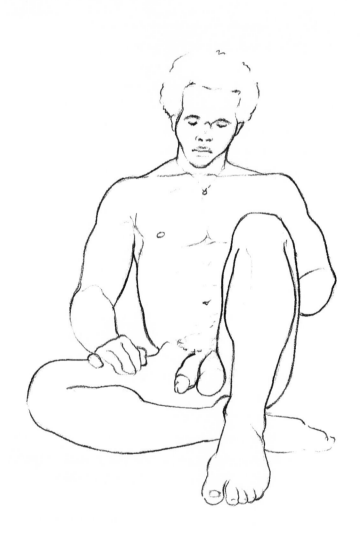

III.

"So, if I Dreame
I Have You, I Have You"

First I had a dream of water,
    then one of rotting.
Your eyes, loosened from their arches,
    were salt ponds, sinking,
and your lips opened like a sluice:
    I failed to follow
the juice where it ran down, rinsing
    a deeper hollow.

The decaying dream worked upward—
    this time I could not
bear to see a jelly taking
    your face, fast, away.
But waking, I extol waking,
    for I cannot call
you to mind without energy:
    movements of making.

I have the will to win over
    rot and water both,
to recover dreams by turning
    them true, thus earning
back what I spent by night. Coming
    is a coming to,
learning by the body's wet spoil
    to endure morning.

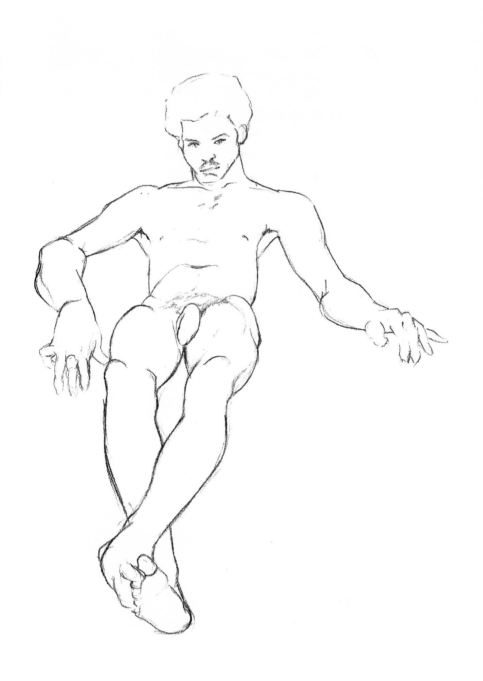

The Shepherd Corydon

Having for some time heard
Nightly in low places
Of incomparable
Creatures that had been hung
Imaginatively
On my heart, disguising
There the boring body
Of a poor imposter,
Having attended to
Whatever bad rumors
Ran among your hopes as
In your most hopeless fears,
You must have expected
The hooded Basilisk
Itself, or the Hydra
Whose rubbery heads are
Likely to penetrate
Anywhere, and supposed
At least the Chimaera
(Which is known for its frauds)
To be among the stale
Myths of a monstrous me.

And this was a mistake.
Later, when you were so
Warmly obliged to give
Away your old fancies,
Was it not difficult
To face the hard choices,
Hating as you did to
Abandon the legend,

The crumbled fairy tales,
In favor of one fact—-
The raw rough animal?

Where and to what purpose
Was the story then? Where,
Finding yourself at last
Here, down, and darkened by
A furious human
Creature in a foreign
Skin—-where was the bright news,
The chronicle of day?

On the sighing bed, boy,
Something changes the past.
Fictions, even yours, turn
Over and expose. You
Became the myth I was
The moment that I came;
More collapsed with the warm
Deceit than is to be
Recovered: Glaucon or
Antinous—-someone
Other!

And terrible
That I, no magic left
Now, by daylight, discover
You, dead, anonymous
After the night, and cold
In your flesh against me . . .

Saturday Morning

Beds are made close to a wall
    flat
Against the blank places.
This is so that most faces
Can turn away from all
    that.

If I turn, the time swarms.
    Word
Of mouth carries the message
Up and down the soft passage
From a hive that hums
    hard.

I am not lonely here:
    fear
Dissolves in mirrors, some
Dangers melt like sweet salve
On a wound. You must have
    come.

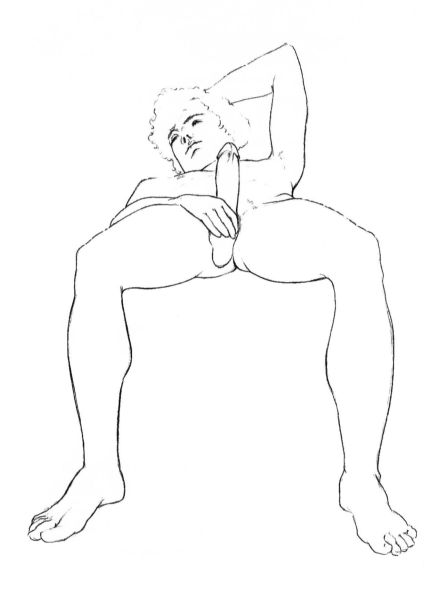

My Last Hustler

. . . all smiles stopped

When "Brad" is lying naked, or rather naked is lying
in wait for whatever those he refers to as clients require
by way of what *they* refer to as satisfaction, denying
himself the distraction of alcohol or amyl, there appears
in his eyes no flicker of shame, no flare of shameless desire,
and what tribute he is paid finds him neither tender nor fierce.

On a bed above suspicion, creases in obviously fresh
linen still mapping a surface only a little creamier than
the creaseless hills and hollows of his compliant flesh,
Brad will extend himself (as the graphic saying goes)
and the upper hand—always his—will push into place *the man
who happens to be there* till happening comes to blows

(another saying you now more fully grasp): full-blown,
Brad will prepare himself, though not precipitately,
for the grateful-kisses stage; he offers cheek and chin
but objects to undergoing your accolade on his mouth:
he has endured such homage too early, too often, too lately,
and for all his boyish ways Brad is not wholly a youth.

Routines on some arduous rigging, however, can restore
him to himself in mirrors, every which way surrounded
by no more than what he seems and mercifully *by no more*.
Booked by a merciless Service for a thousand afternoons,
Brad will become the needs of his "regulars" confounded
by his indifferent regard, by his regardless expense . . .

Take him—young faithful!—there and then. Marvel! praise!
Fond though your touch may be and truly feeling your tact,
yet a mocking echo returns—remote, vague, blasé—
of Every Future Caress, so very like your own!
However entranced the scene you make (the two of you act
as one to all appearance, but one is always alone),

derision will come to mind, or to matter over mind:
the folly, in carnal collusion, of mere presented *skill*.
Undone, played out, discharged, one insight you will have gained
which cannot for all these ardent lapses be gainsaid
—even his murmured subsidence an exercise of will—
is the sudden absolute knowledge Brad would rather be dead.

Domesticities

We ate from the dish of eyes
and as eyes met, making out
light by darkness, we hungered:
      the dish is a questioning of the dish.

We drank from the cup of hands
and as hands met, reaching down
for what was up, we thirsted:
      the cup is a questioning of the cup.

We slept in the bed of flesh
and as flesh met, melting back
to the lost action, we kept
      forgiving, and for good: no questions asked.

RICHARD HOWARD was born in 1929 in Cleveland, Ohio, and studied at Columbia University and at the Sorbonne. After working for several years as a lexicographer, he became a translator from the French and has published more than 150 translations, including books by Gide, Giraudoux, Cocteau, Camus, DeBeauvoir, DeGaulle, Breton, Barthes, RobbeGrillet, Cioran, Claude Simon, and Baudelaire's *Fleurs du Mal*, for which he received the National Book Award in translation in 1983. In 1970 he was awarded the Pulitzer Prize for his third book of poems, *Untitled Subjects*, and in 1995 was a finalist for the National Book Award for his tenth book of poems, *Like Most Revelations*. He is a member of the American Academy and Institute of Arts and Letters, a Chancellor of the Academy of American Poets, and Professor at the School of the Arts at Columbia University.

JOHN BUTTON (1929-1982) was born in San Francisco and had his first exhibition of paintings with the Tibor de Nagy Gallery in 1956. His work has been exhibited widely in galleries and is in the permanent collection of many museums throughout the United States including the Metropolitan Museum of Art, the Museum of Modern Art and the Hirshhorn Museum and Sculpture Garden. He taught painting and drawing at the School of Visual Arts in New York, and at the Graduate School of Fine Arts at University of Pennsylvania.

The text of this book is set in Sabon typeface.
Five-hundred copies were printed by McNaughton & Gunn, Inc.
in Saline, Michigan. It was edited by Eric Brown
and designed by Paul Lafortezza.